# Sharing for Sheep

Zanna Davidson

Illustrated by
Alison Friend

Designed by Tabitha Blore
Edited by Lesley Sims

Did you know, when you're not looking...
sheep are knitting lots of things...

From hats
to scarves
to mittens...
...to toys
and woolly wings!

Right now they're **extra** busy,
because they're on a mission.
Each sheep is trying hard to win…

THE KNITTING COMPETITION!

They have from **dawn** till **sunset**
to knit the BEST they can.
And one sheep in particular
has a **very** cunning plan.

**Ernie's** trying to knit a blanket...

My biggest one so far.
And when I'm done, I will have proved
that **I'M** the knitting star!

But unbeknownst to Ernie
Olive's had the same idea.
My blanket's sure to be the best.
How everyone will cheer!

All day their needles go click-clack!

Olive's making final touches.
"Hooray! I'm nearly there!"
But then she glances over –
and cries out in **GREAT DESPAIR!**

They're knitting from
ONE BALL OF YARN!
There isn't any more!

There's only
ONE THING for it...

Let's have a
TUG-OF-WAR!

"I need this yarn," cries Ernie,
"or my blanket won't be done."

Olive snorts and shakes her head,
**"You're not the ONLY one!"**

They **stamp** their feet.

They **grit** their teeth.

They **stare** with narrowed eyes.

I DESERVE to win this CONTEST!
I REALLY want that prize!

Just then the wind starts blowing hard.
A bird tweets out,
BEWARE!
The yarn's all knotty. It goes…
SNAP!
and flies off through the air.

It sails down the hillside.
It whizzes over trees.
As both sheep run, they bellow out,

The ball has reached the town now.

It's bounced into a store.

Both sheep come tumbling after…

…and get wedged inside the door.

The yarn's landed in the basket
of a lady in high heels.

Olive
follows
stealthily…

They jump on board a scooter.
And catch up with the bus.

I'm not so sure we're welcome here...
We're causing quite a fuss!

They grab the yarn. It's time to leave…
They take a mighty

# LEAP!

The people on the bus cry out,
"There go two flying sheep!"

They cannon through a thorny hedge.
(Olive's lost her hat.)

And then they land together, with a loud and muddy

SPLAT!

Both sheep are in a soggy mess.
They sit there, simply staring.
"Do you think it's time…" they say,
"for us to think of… **sharing**?"

"I'd like that!" says a squeaky voice.
Out peeps a little mouse.

So Olive hands some over.

But then they meet a pair of ducks,
who beg some for their nest.

And on it goes…

the whole way home…

...till the yarn has gone completely!

And as the sun sets in the sky,
they both share one more time...
They stitch and sew their blankets up.
But can they win first prize?

Of course they win!



Olive smiles at Ernie. "Not only have we won,
we've made a blanket big enough…"

"So there's room for
EVERYONE!"

First published in 2023 by Usborne Publishing Limited, 83-85 Saffron Hill,
London EC1N 8RT, United Kingdom. usborne.com

Design Manager: Nicola Butler    Digital manipulation: John Russell